VALE AVE

NEW DIRECTIONS POETRY PAMPHLETS

#1   Susan Howe: *Sorting Facts; or, Nineteen Ways of Looking at Marker*

#2   Lydia Davis / Eliot Weinberger: *Two American Scenes*

#3   Bernadette Mayer: *The Helens of Troy, NY*

#4   Sylvia Legris: *Pneumatic Antiphonal*

#5   Nathaniel Tarn: *The Beautiful Contradictions*

#6   Alejandra Pizarnik: *A Musical Hell*

#7   H. D.: *Vale Ave*

#8   Forrest Gander: *Eiko & Koma*

forthcoming

#9   Lawrence Ferlinghetti: *Blasts Cries Laughter*

#10   Osama Alomar: *Fullblood Arabian*

#11   Oliverio Girondo: *Poems to Read on a Streetcar*

#12   *Fifteen Iraqi Poets* (ed. Dunya Mikhail)

H. D.

VALE AVE

NEW DIRECTIONS POETRY PAMPHLET #7

NOTE ON THE TEXT

This edition of *Vale Ave* was first published by Black Swan Books in 1992, and is based on H.D.'s corrected final draft of the poem in the American Literature Collection of The Beinecke Library, Yale University. An earlier, incomplete version of the poem appeared in *New Directions 44* (1982). Sections V and XXXVII appeared in *Poetry* (1957) and Section XVIII in *The Atlantic* (1958).

Cover design by Office of Paul Sahre
Interior design by Erik Rieselbach
Manufactured in the United States of America
New Directions Books are printed on acid-free paper.
First published as New Directions Poetry Pamphlet #7 in 2013
Published simultaneously in Canada by Penguin Books Canada Limited

Library of Congress Cataloging-in-Publication Data
H. D. (Hilda Doolittle), 1886–1961.
Vale ave / H.D.
pages ; cm. — (New Directions poetry pamphlet ; #7)
ISBN 978-0-8112-2107-8 (acid-free paper)
I. Title.
PS3507.O726V35 2013
811'.52—dc23

2013005431

10 9 8 7 6 5 4 3 2 1

New Directions Books are published for James Laughlin
by New Directions Publishing Corporation
80 Eighth Avenue, New York, NY 10011

To: Amico.
Küsnacht, Spring 1957

This sequence introduces Adam's first wife, Lilith. Is she the Serpent who tests the *androgynat primordial*? Serpent (*saraph*), it is said, has the same root derivation as Seraph, so Lilith may be Serpent or Seraph, as Adam, whom we invoke as Lucifer, the Lightbringer, in his pre-Eve manifestation, may be Angel or Devil.

The Lucifer-Lilith, Adam-Eve formula may be applied to all men and women, though here we follow the *processus* through the characters of Elizabeth and Sir Walter, meeting and parting, *Vale Ave*, through time—specifically, late Rome, dynastic Egypt, legendary Provence, early seventeenth-century England, and contemporary London. She is the niece of the Elizabethan poet and alchemist Sir Edward Dyer. Sir Walter secretly and mysteriously becomes her lover during the last months of his life in the Tower of London. After his death, Elizabeth recalls him to her, through her uncle's Art and through the alchemy of memory. Sir Walter was himself an alchemist, as history tells us, and Elizabeth identifies herself with him, although:

> I hardly knew my Lord, true we had met
> in sudden frenzy, parted in the dark,
> and all the rest was mystery and a portent.

Mystery and a portent, yes, but at the same time, there is Resurrection and the hope of Paradise.

I

We would name you Light-bearer,
pre-Adamic, of the sacred *Luciferum*,

no Dark Majesty but Light-bringer,
an Angel as God first created you,

for it is true that I called to you,
it is true that you answered,

"it was no serpent that God cursed,
it was Adam's first wife, Lilith,

who spoke in the Tree"; was Lucifer, Adam,
was Adam, Lucifer, torn asunder,

one Adam for Eve, one for Lilith,
his first wife, a being, an entity

born of no man-rib but a Tree;
Lucifer and Lilith, to taste no bitter fruit,

nor toil nor bear children,
but to remember, only to remember . . .

II

"Cursed shall be she,
the Voice within the Tree,"
but for how long?

True, I was a long time there,
Carthage, Rome, Tyre,
while you ploughed the earth, implacable,

Hannibal, Caesar, Martel;
those chains could never hold,
the pit was never closed,

but a volcano made earth uninhabitable,
here, there; there, here;
but still enchantment rose

out of the sea, when in the centurion's tent,
or by the dunes, or in a fisher's hut,
following inexorable destiny, we met.

III

For us, no open door
to hearth and the hearth-fire,
the moment before, the long rest after,

but immediacy, urgency—awake? asleep?—
a chasm, a cave, a monstrous fissure
in time, a breaking of law,

time-sequence, star-sequence;
the sun stands still,
the moon unveiled, revealed,

forgets to draw the tides;
the earth will shiver and break
if we hesitate—asleep? awake?

IV

Yet sometimes, I would sweep the floor,
I would put daisies in a tumbler,
I would have long dreams before, long daydreams after,

there would be no gauntleted knock on the door,
or tap-tap with a riding crop,
no galloping here and back,

but the latch would softly lift,
would softly fall,
dusk would come slowly,

and even dusk could wait
till night encompassed us;
dawn would come gracious, not too soon,

day would come late,
and the next day and the next,
while I found pansies to take the place of daisies,

and a spray of apple blossom after that,
no calendar of fevered hours,
Carthago delenda est and the Tyrian night.

V

O, we were penitent enough, God knows,
you wore the Nessus' tunic,
I, the rose with nails for petals,

underneath my robe; I pressed
the seven swords of Mary to my heart,
within the hollow of my wounded breasts;

I walked, numb with the incense,
never passed a friar or priest or brother,
but my glance fell to the pavement,

but the very stones of the cathedral floor
bore imprint of your sandals;
I must close my eyes or stare

at the rose window, but the rose betrayed,
the glow of green and azure set aflame
the row of kings and saints along the wall,

the stone-story of Creation and the Fall;
O, we were penitent enough, God knows,
but how revoke decrees made long ago?

VI

The candle swells with weight of its own fervor,
the melting wax runs down,
to fill the hollow of the candleholder,

and as it flames with headier heat and headier,
it seems to blaze with iridescent splendor
that I may never look upon,

prostrated as I am, in adoration;
the lashes of my eyes are wet,
my swollen eyelids burn;

dear Lord, how long can I endure,
my cold hands clasped, my numb knees
frozen on this chapel floor?

VII

Go now, my love, the cock has crowed again,
go now, my love, dawn touches the windowframe,
go now, my love, your face is haggard and worn,

tell to your waiting brothers, you had sworn
to do your triple penance, say, all night long,
you flayed your worn flesh, Our Lord witnessed it;

go, go my love, I join my sisters now,
trembling and weak; dear sister, one will say,
you must not try the flesh unutterably,

but if I must, I must, I'll answer her;
go now, for it is day, or soon will be,
and we will take our place within the row

of kneeling worshipers and penitents,
and we will vow again, our ancient vow,
at Matins; it is day, go, go.

VIII

Our ancient vow—within the purple tent,
I lay alone; he left a goblet (spiced with—what?)
within my reach; all day the village burned;

have he and his few strength to drive them back,
or will they throng, beasts in their wild-beast pelts,
great bearded giants with their threatening horns,

will they swoop and tear me, helpless, hapless here,
will they stare and laugh,
see what has stricken Rome,

will they leer and ask in their barbaric speech,
which is best, to take her in a cage
or burn her here; will they keep

a naked, unkempt Lilith for a show
for witches and young women with fair hair?
Will he return? I have not strength to stand.

IX

Keep Lilith in a cage, curse Lilith in a Tree?
no; no barbaric hordes nor gods can yet prevail
against the law that drags the snail across the grass,

that turns the falcon from his course,
that drives the lion until he finds
the lioness within the cave;

men gave new names to us, many names, fabulous,
but Lilith was the first that God cursed outright,
and Lucifer's became that sinister name,

while man himself rebelled and fabricated meteor and flame,
such as the thunder once alone proclaimed,
"death-dealing such as this, comes but from God";

could *aves* and could prayers control
these man-made meteors, God knows
I would be penitent enough and crawl

in sackcloth on my bleeding knees,
but those prayers are worn threadbare;
there must be others, bright with vivid fire,

revitalizing, luminous, life-bearing
and light-bringing, to compel a Star, Lucifer,
to return and save mankind.

X

"They drive them past the riverbank," he said;
I must have slept, the air was soft and cool,
he stood in his blue tunic; had he come

some hour or some half-hour before I woke?
"does Octavius keep your armor in his tent?"
he said, "I let Octavius take my place,"

(he never left his men), "and are there others here?"
I asked; "they will come later," and he took the goblet
and turned it slowly, "then, you swallowed this?"

"perhaps, I can't remember"; "there was only
the poppy-juice, the opiate in the wine,
I left for sleep"; "and you are tired," I said;

"no, never half so glad, so wide awake," he led
me to the open space before the tent, and far I saw and far,
the peaceful contour of the winding river,

and levels where the villages had been;
it must have rained, there was no smoke,
no breath of smoldering timbers, it was clear

and stars were as snow drifting in mid-air . . .
we seemed one flambeau for the world to see,
we did not even know that we were dead.

XI

And those we left? Hermas comes first,
he made a garden on the Aventine;
my Lord, how is it, I remember this,

for suddenly (whose fault?) we find ourselves
crowded against a bulwark on a wharf,
buffeted by alien winds—take cover—

whose the shout—whose ships—whose men,
my Lord, why are we here—why do you shudder—
am I stronger then, than you

who played the god before all men?
where are we—and what threatens—
are you the enemy, are they seeking you

with lantern on the quay
and sentries on the breakwater?
O, do not tear yourself away,

for if they take you, I am lost again;
where did we come from—how did we meet here—
where have you gone—

dear Lord, and is this all that I have left,
only this empty, old discarded cloak?
my alien garments weigh my limbs like lead,

when I would run—
Ave Maria—save us,
Christ who saves.

XII

It filtered through, though it was lies, I knew,
he had been stretched upon the rack and tried,
condemned and died;

"no, no, he was beheaded; he did not swing
at Tyburn, as they say," "but quiet, quiet, Peter,
the Lady Elizabeth may overhear";

"tell her to go—some saw her on the quay—
and go yourself, I'll stay on at the Tower,"
(I crouched upon the landing of the upper stair),

"the gates are closed or will be before day,
I have the Tower passes and the key; Agatha, go";
"they will not want us, Peter, at the Manor,

with all this talk of plague"; "but they are
Christian folk and she is kin, make ready,
she is weak, some say, with child,

although her Lord left here, a year ago—"
—"hist—he returned and made a secret visit,
on the Queen's business—" "—you know he died of fever,

in New Spain"; "no matter, how can I drag her away;
to her, the very paving stones are sacred
and London is a holy city to her."

XIII

I can not remember, only that my name
was Elizabeth Dyer; I can not remember my husband,
only my lover; I faintly remember old nurse Agatha

and her husband, who had been our house-servant
and now carried a halberd at the Tower;
I can not remember how we got away,

I can remember a dead child but I never saw it,
and maybe, it wasn't dead, after all,
I was too ill to remember;

Agatha was herself, a Tower, things were hidden
under flowing mantles, in those days,
and strange, alien farthingales, and Agatha put me to bed, anyway;

I was delirious and I talked (she said) of a purple tent,
and men with horns (devils, she thought, I meant)
and stars and lilies and the Aventine.

XIV

I had my mother's Missal, but the prayers
fluttered against the dark and broke and fell,
for this too, was anathema and cursed,

the good Queen had instructed all of us,
to do away with painted images,
the breviary and the Latin and the Mass;

but there were furtive, secret worshipers,
we were suspect, in that I shared the curse
that fell upon my Lord and atheists;

Hieronymos, pity us, Agnes, Lucy, help;
the very names were potent but they fluttered,
fell and broke, like aimless birds, lost

on a continent that lured them north,
that later, in the winter, would have drawn them back
to sun and sand, the Mystery and Egypt.

XV

I hardly knew my Lord, true we had met
in sudden frenzy, parted in the dark,
and all the rest was mystery and a portent;

none had stood higher in the Queen's respect,
name England and you know his name,
Agatha sheltered us, he came and went;

no shadow followed us until the last;
I drew him to me through my uncle's Art,
though I knew little of it, at his death,

he named the Seraphim, the future would encompass us,
he said, separate yet together with their wings;
"Sir Edward Dyer's Niece?

"you mean that Edward Dyer who was disgraced?
an alchemist who told the Queen the truth?
but where is she?" somehow he found me out;

perhaps it was not difficult, "her name, her reputation?"
"almost a nun; she lives with two old servants
near the Tower; her husband's in New Spain."

XVI

They spoke his name across the candles,
the goblets stood unmoving on the table
and the table stood and those same cups

I always loved, the fruit bowl, the decanter;
the candleflames burned straight, they never moved,
I thought an earthquake shook the house

but it was I who trembled when my uncle spoke,
(the candleflames burned straight, they never moved),
"you must have heard talk of this in the town";

my cousin answered, "let her forget the town—
they said, he bribed the gatekeepers,
and came and went out of the Tower,

but never far; they even say
he could have got away by sea,
but honored his *parole*";

(and now the wind was beating in my face
and it was dark, and I was clutching at an empty cloak,
and salt of my tears mingled with its salt);

I think I thanked my cousin for he broke an apple,
I always thought this was a clever trick
when we were children;

I think he smiled,
remembering my past effort and defeat;
"Lizeth," he said, "drink your red wine, eat this."

XVII

Lizeth? was Lizeth, Lilith in the Tree?
anger had drawn me back and out of time,
but now, I see in-time and passionately;

I would recall the symbols, name the Powers,
invoke the Angels, Tetragrammaton;
I am far from her now, but she is near,

chalking her circle with its letters on the attic floor;
step in it, Lizeth, dare Elizabeth Dyer,
to ponder on the secrets, writ in fire,

in the old book you found in the oak chest;
"our uncle's book," the cousin said and laughed,
"for this, he was disgraced," and read a list

of names, "exciting stuff—
let's call up Lucifer—do you remember how
we ran away and hid here, long ago?"

XVIII

He dragged me through the hedge,
"you used to laugh," he said, "Lizeth,
laugh and forget, be glad";

he kissed my face, "my flower, you are too pale,
I'll get you eglantine and the red pinks,
that we called sops-in-wine—do you remember?"

a bird whistled and a bird replied,
"so you see, everywhere, two and two," he said
"under the blossoming trees, the chestnut-spire,

the pear, you must have missed the garden,
that long year, London was always drear";
he drew me down beside him on the grass,

and he unfastened shoulder-clasp and band,
and cupped my breasts within his firm young hands,
"so here," he said, "are peonies—and here—no rose is half so dear."

XIX

Could I forget, would I forget?
Lucifer, you have queens about you now,
Helen and Guinevere; Semiramis

orders her servants to direct the prow
toward Egypt—is it Egypt?
I will know tonight, when I escape

and stand within my circle; I marked it out
at first, but now it is invisible,
though its letters, copied from my uncle's book,

shine in the darkness, to invoke the Sephirs;
I would espouse your cause and find it good,
for I have understood at last,

the hints and pauses of our visitors,
the sudden turn the talk takes
whenever I appear, but shameless or inspired,

I hear, waiting a moment by the open door,
"he had strange traffic with daemonic powers"
they said, "and spirits of the dead."

XX

His was not lover's talk, like Hugh's,
only the long, long stare by day,
with curtains drawn, or in the firelit dusk,
or by the candles, on the dressing table;

he flung his hat and cloak upon a chair,
and paced the length of the small room
and turned and always said, "I must go soon";
the room was not so small, it was the bed,

with crimson covers, an old bed from home
that took the space, but still there were
those narrow corridors, one at the foot,
one between bed and window, one by the door;

so he paced the floor, around, across, across,
around and back, until I fell,
driven as by a prowling lion or panther,
upon the crimson cover of the bed.

XXI

When Hugh's away at sea, I climb the stair,
the triangles and hexagons have grown dim;
the pentagon, the circle and the cross

have disappeared, but they are all inscribed
within my heart, the Tree of Life or Trees,
the pathways and the planets with their signs;

I can follow on from Mars to Venus,
to Jupiter, to Saturn, to the Crown, *Kether,*
and down again past *Daath,* past Mercury

to the core and root, *Malkuth,*
and on past the Dark Queen upon the throne,
Beth is her name or letter, after *Aleph,*

the priest or the magician by the altar;
there are the old prints in my uncle's book,
but I need not consult them any more;

I know one of the Trees is Rigor, one is Mercy,
and in between the two, the Tree of balance, equilibrium
leads on to Beauty, *Tiphereth,* the Sun.

XXII

For all the thrones and letters spell one story,
and only one, Love is the altar that we burn upon;

did he find that, after his frantic quest,
experiments, his journeys and the search

everywhere in old books, Latin and Hebrew texts?
Hugh helped when he was here, he told me how

they kept a sanctum in his house, above the river,
with astrolabe and crucible and a group,

dedicated to a secret cult of Night;
we talked of this and of our uncle's alchemy

and his disgrace; "find out for me what it was all about,"
I asked my cousin with false negligence,

"I want to know, I'll put away the book,
I promise not to read it any more,

or only now and then, consult it for a name
that comes and goes, not quite remembered,

and not quite forgot" (I laughed)
"that I must exorcise."

XXIII

"Now, tell me everything, Hugh, everything,"
"no woman should explore these devious rites,
no girl like you";

"our uncle blessed me with the angels' names
I found them in the book and now it's clear,
he watches over us, he knows—"

"knows what?" "the Secret and the Sanctum,
how we met—I did not really know his name
till Agatha and Peter spoke of it,

after they took him; then I saw the part
he played in history, learned the plot;
you yourself spoke of this,

one night across the candles, at the table,
he honored his *parole*, you said—"
"my Lizeth, are you mad?"

"he came and went—you yourself said,
he bribed the gatekeepers, you yourself said,
he came and went, but never far—"

"but this was an impostor—" "no, no—for Peter knew him—"
"knew Sir Walter?" "O, do not speak the name,
perhaps another, an angel took his shape—"

"you mean a devil—" "but angels manifest sometimes
in forms of men—" "better it was Sir Walter
than your delirium of angels in men's forms."

XXIV

Tiphereth is beauty in that book,
the center and the Sun, an altar in the temple,
the shadow outline of an upright man;

can this be blasphemy? then what is beauty?
it is a square room and a bed within,
a square within a square, geometry,

the absolute answer to all alchemy;
he prowls along the narrow corridors,
at the foot, the bedside and the other side,

and as I lie waiting, I seem to see
myself, worshiping at the altar;
Semiramis, did I say, orders her servants

to direct the prow toward Egypt?
that was fantasy, but we are here;
this is Elizabeth Dyer,

we are in-time, today,
the past can neither add nor take away
from that small room, a square within a square.

XXV

The Tree, the Temple and the upright Man,
the square, the circle and add to the five,
the Oracle, my uncle's Seraphim;

he said the future would encompass us,
separate yet together, with their wings;
I do not need to seek their names,

their letters and their numbers in the book,
for they are ONE, yet doubled, two and two, a host
to sweep us to God's throne—and I am lost—

spare me myself, my small identity, I pray,
who should submit, soar higher, caught away;
spare me my name, Elizabeth, spare me his,

although he never said Lady Elizabeth,
nor I, Sir Walter—dear Lord,
do I remember now that time "before"—

for galleys crash and fire is flung,
and I again am standing on a wharf,
watching a tall mast slowly disappear.

XXVI

The past can neither add nor take away, I said,
but now "before" and "after" challenge each other,
a satrap or a monk with sunken eyes,

a memory of a purple sleeve, a memory of bliss,
a memory of repentance and slow death,
a memory of burning censers and the sulphur fumes

that vainly choke the half dead; there is hope;
there is no hope, the cart is at the door,
you can not sort them out; leave them

and nail them in, or take the lot?
whose is the voice, what executioner
condemns us all together?

XXVII

I am a ghost tending a little flame,
but one spark may ignite the host
of invisible Seraphim so that they

may visibly manifest on earth to men;
I speak his name, a thousand men appear,
or would if they could hear;

he could have ruled the realm, the world,
only he chose the way of love, Elizabeth (another, not the Queen)
and found himself (and with her) in the Tower;

that was his earlier plight, the later
was longer—I heard the story of his short release,
of his return, then of his death;

maybe my part was sheer delirium,
as Hugh once said; maybe it was an angel
that paced the corridors about my bed;

maybe it was an angel in my room,
("my Lizeth—are you mad?")
or maybe as Hugh said, it was a devil.

XXVIII

It needed fire to generate remembrance,
Love was the *primum mobile*, the mediator,
Carthage, Rome, Tyre,

and on to the Cathedral's apse and nave
and the flesh crucified, until
remembrance brought us to this hour,

in which I strive, with or without
the litany and prayers, to save identity,
the Man—Angel or Devil.

XXIX

I do go back and clutch my precious book
and warm it at my breast,
it is the child I lost;

O infinite grace—my uncle granted me
this blessing and this peace,
here is a great sun, set between the trees

of Paradise, those same trees
with names of God, the same God
and yet other, some seventy names or more,

inscribed in the circumference of this Flower;
I dare not read them, printed on the page,
later, I'll light my candle, kneel and seek

the numbers and the names upon the chart,
divided round the circle of the year,
so one can find the special Angel

and God's special name
that guides the soul from birth;
I know his birthday and the day he died,

and my name on the chart lies not so far from his;
Azriel who saw him die, now let me live
to honor and to serve the names of God.

XXX

He honored his *parole* and loved,
and that has saved his soul and mine;

better the dim, sweet sanctuary of my room
and ignorance (mine) of his activity

with crucibles and astrolabes, of which they spoke,
his traffic with daemonic powers and spirits of the dead;

Lilith and Lucifer—let them not be lost,
O God of more than seventy names

and attributes of justice—let us keep these,
as symbols of our meeting, for his death

redeemed us, spared us, made the memory
of a little room, one of the aspects of eternity,

one of the stations, measured in that Sun
by rays from the circumference,

with numbers that again are found
in Paradise, upon the leaves;

we were one number; separate, we are two
upon the Tree of Heaven, *Sephirothique.*

XXXI

Julius come back, Julius come back,
I flamed too high and now I toss with fever,

there was a purple tent, there was a river,
there was real terror of barbaric hosts,

physical fear, but there was the escape,
the cup within my reach; even as you turned

to speak, before you parted the tent folds,
you said, "keep the wine till the last," and *vale,*

and paused with the fold lifted like a banner,
to add *ave* and dropped the folds and went;

the names I whispered on my knees,
the prayers I sent to heaven had no place there;

the world has punished us enough,
peace, peace, there were no Tower, no severed head,

peace, peace, there was no plague, penance, redemption,
but only at the last, your voice that said *ave.*

XXXII

"You can not beat them back, the garrisons are weak,
stay here, let Julia rest here in the garden,

Rome is doomed anyway, enjoy today today,
you are not Caesar, our great ancestor;

they won't get here tomorrow or next year,
or the year after, the legions are on guard about the walls,

there is enough to do here in the city,
see, Julia begs you stay," and Hermas put his arm

about my shoulder, "you almost disappear
among the lilies, in this white and silver";

O Hermas, comforter, you would have kept me there,
but I must disappear, though not among your lilies;

"a hunting trip? you can't get past the gates—"
"Octavius will help"— "Julia, you're mad"—

it was a simple matter after all,
and all discretion for the *laticlave*.

XXXIII

It was cool even amidst the furor,
our tent was set apart, with Octavius

always near to sound the alert
and help him with his armor;

within my thought, I prayed the Dioscuri,
no marble set in Hermas' corridor,

but beings in reality and near;
give us a Ship, we'll sail down this wide river,

the sea is not so far, I would forget
anxiety and ceaseless threat and war,

for we would found a City, greater
and with more power, even than ancient Rome.

XXXIV

No god set in an alcove, no god upon a plinth,
no plain Adonis, no slain Hyacinth,

for none slays Love, inconsequent and unpredictable,
he comes—how, no man knows,

and all the rest is leveled to the ground,
the city walls, the fortress and the Tower;

we stand alone, Julius and Julia,
the past, the future and the present, one;

what if we meet and do not know each other?
we'll meet again—we talked philosophy, Lucretius, Plato;

what if we meet, and one has gone the right,
the other on the lefthand path?

so we discussed the Eastern mysteries,
Pythagoras and rebirth; how often have we met like this,

how often have we separated, torn apart
in hate, bitterness and in disgrace?

XXXV

Ave and *vale*, but the parting came
before the greeting, it was *vale, ave,*

keep the wine till the last,
I hold this cup, I need not taste this sleep,

I hold the globe, as once so long ago
(or once, some centuries later),

I clutched the apple in my helpless hands
and could not break it—who would break this sphere,

this perfect crystal of reflected rose and red
and purple of the sanctuary, the tent folds,

or long ago (or was it centuries later?)
the crimson cover of an ark, a bed,

Sanctum Sanctorum where a stranger lay,
who always flung his cloak upon a chair,

and paced the room in urgency and fever,
and always said, "I must go soon."

XXXVI

The best wine came last, as we learnt long ago,
(or was it centuries later?) at the marriage feast;

the best will come, I know, when I drink this,
who knows, my Lord, how long before we meet?

what claims you now? do you instruct
new legions, do you plan a sudden sortie

on the race of man, and on the peril
of the man-made meteors?

would you destroy the whole to build again
the radiant city where man walks with man,

in confidence, invoking the benign
Omnipotence, who yet explains the pattern,

so we see even the smallest act,
in its proportion and significance;

but no—stay as you are a little longer,
stay as you are for years, for centuries,

and give me time to reinvoke the past
and read the future in this gazing glass,

this crystal of reflected rose and red,
for the best wine came last.

XXXVII

Now there are gold reflections on the water,
how old am I and how have the years passed?

I do not know your age nor mine, nor when you died,
I only know your stark, hypnotic eyes

are different and other eyes meet mine, amber and fire,
in the changed content of the gazing glass;

O, I am old, old, old and my cold hand
clutches my shawl about my shivering shoulders,

I have no power against this bitter cold,
this weakness and this trembling, I am old;

who am I, why do I wait here, what have I lost?
nothing or everything but I gain this,

an image in the sacred lotus pool,
a hand that hesitates to break

the lily from the lily stalk and spoil
what may be vision of a Pharaoh's face.

XXXVIII

"She is not grown, my Lord, a child
and without grace," an arm about my shoulder,

a voice—a gardener or a temple servant (Hermas?),
a dark, ironic face, a gesture and a glance,

the sound of metal on the marble pavement,
the bronze-edged sandal of a charioteer?

a soldier, captain or mere household-keeper,
one of the Pharaoh's men but not the Pharaoh,

one of the palace guard, not greater
than my protector, scribe and foster-father;

"later, my Lord, review the temple dancers
with me, there are new girls from Cos

and overseas, brought back since you last left;
my Lord, I am your servant,

and your campaign," he bowed,
"we learn, was most felicitous."

XXXIX

Then or much later, then or earlier,
then when time paused, for even time must pause

at a command—whose?—neither god nor Pharaoh
can subdue his stride, can laugh at time, the tyrant

and his scythe; reap armies, populations, whet your scimitar,
begin again on hoplites and the legions, even Alexander

stops at the horizon, but not we; there is a brazier
in a corridor, there is a blue cloth slung across a door,

there is the sound of curtain rings along the rod,
that then slide back and the blue curtain falls in its old folds,

and we are standing on a mosaic floor,
whose pattern is familiar, fish in water,

birds in the reeds, and a papyrus scroll
hangs on the wall; I see them there forever,

nor need turn and read the inscription
and translate the letters—for he can not read—

no business of a soldier—call a scribe—
but there are other symbols which he knows and sees,

and turns to appraise—one purple lily
in an alabaster vase.

XL

If there is urgency, there is no fear,
hail, yes, but not farewell,

Amenti flowered long before Eden's tree;
his hand invites the *delta* underneath

the half-transparent folds of the soft pleats,
and does not tear but draws the veil aside,

then both his hands grasp my bare thighs,
and clutch and tighten, bird claws or a beast

that would tear open, tear apart, but keep
the appetite at bay, to gratify a greater hunger

or to anticipate deeper enjoyment;
yet his commanding knees keep my knees locked,

even while his virility soothes and quickens,
till in agony, my own hands clutch and tear,

and my lips part, as he releases me,
and my famished mouth opens

and knows his hunger and his power;
and this is the achievement and we know the answer

to ritual and to all philosophy,
in the appeasement of the ravished flower.

XLI

I must have married Hugh; the house belongs to me,
the fields, the little river; visitors come and go,

even the Lady Abbess, a niece or daughter
of an old friend of my mother;

she is aristocratic and at ease but always says,
"Lady Elizabeth belongs to us;

she would have more leisure and more peace
at our Retreat," and she begs me come

not far across the fields, to Matins or Compline;
I smile apology and I decline,

remembering the old days and the old loyalties;
she does not know how once and feverishly,

I read my Missal till the pages faded
and the *Aves* cried, "it is another *Ave* that you seek,

a prayer within a prayer,
let life not spoil the hope of Paradise."

XLII

O, that was long ago, the purple lily,
and that was long ago, the *vale, ave,*

and that was long, long after, but the same
hunger, the same desire, the same appeasement,

in London, near the Tower, "my Lizeth, are you mad?"
for years, I faced Sir Hugh across the table,

after his father's death, for years, I spoke with gentlefolk
and kind, Hugh's cousins and our neighbors,

for years, I said, "when Hugh comes back,"
wearing the gowns he chose; a visitor

would look askance at Lady Elizabeth,
the ancient in her outmoded dress,

even although they had prepared the stranger,
"her husband's death—the shock—his ship *Seaspray*

was lost—you won't remember—off the coast
of Portugal, I think it was—long ago, James was king,

she's old—O, very old—she can't remember
what happened yesterday ..."

XLIII

What happened yesterday? a way of living,
a way of plunging reckless through the fires,

a way of waiting, "O, they'll soon pass over,"
a way of thinking, "where is Phoebe, do you think, Amico,

that one was nearer us or nearer her?
we might have sent her overseas—

if anything should happen—"
the doorbell or the telephone? "O, it's you,

we were just wondering—" "it's all right,
the all-clear's sounded somewhere."

XLIV

What happened yesterday? a field of thorns,
grasp them, they turn to lilies,

the doorbell or the telephone? "O, do come in,"
he flung his hat and coat upon a chair,

it seemed we were familiar, *semblables*,
we were "familiars" and total strangers,

his eyes stared as his eyes had stared before,
nothing was changed, where everything was different,

the eagles and the legions, death and war,
the bronze-edged sandal of a charioteer,

London as always, it was just the same,
the coast guards and the signals and the fire.

XLV

There was no time to dream till it was over,
hail and farewell; there was no time

in which to read the pictures,
the message and the writing on the wall,

true, I transcribed the scroll,
he said he could not read—

no business of a soldier—call a scribe—
I did not know that he saw more and further

than I could ever see—I did not know
that he knew everything, yet waited for an answer

in Egypt, in a sort of trance
of patience and of fury, Oedipus, the King;

I gave the answer though I played the part
of prophetess or Sphinx, unknowingly.

I did not know he was invisible,
like Gyges with the ring.

XLVI

It took a long time to decipher this,
the Mystery, the Writing and the Scroll,

infinity portrayed in simple things,
in courteous answer or abrupt reply,

I read the surface script, it was enough,
no hat, no coat, but gloves flung on a chair,

"I wonder if I left my car in order,"
and he was off, down the three flights of stairs

and back, I waited for him at the door;
"I have less than an hour," he said,

and laid his watch beside him on the table;
he said, "I must rush off to meet my daughter";

what did I know? I poured the tea,
I offered cigarettes, "no, no," and he took up his watch

"now I must go," and this was one of seven short visits
to decipher, seven meetings to decode.

XLVII

I transcribed the scroll, I wrote it out
and then I wrote it over, a palimpsest of course,

but it came clear, at last, I had the answer
or the seven answers to the seven riddles,

the why and why and why—the meetings and the parting
and his anger—it took some time, though five years is not long

to write a story, set in eternity but lived in—England;
I left of course; I traveled to the Tessin from Lausanne,

to Zürich and around and back again,
and I wrote furiously; he got the last of this prose Trilogy,

this record, set in time or fancy-dressed in history,
five years ago, then I had five years left

to break all barriers, to surpass myself
with *Helen and Achilles* . . .

an epic poem? unquestionably that,
I would not trouble him to read the script.

XLVIII

But bitterness sets in, a different sort of bitterness
but the same, the fear of fear that runs within my veins,

the fear of helplessness, of being lost;
O, I have many friends, Phoebe is safe,

I have three grandchildren; O, I have hosts
of friends—letters—the post? there's no anxiety,

is that the catch? let them lie there until I finish this,
I need not run them through, America, Italy, even a German stamp,

England of course; I need not fear to find or not to find
the envelope with the somewhat cramped address

and my name, the postmark not the same, not London now
but somewhere in the country;

O, that was long ago, the fire, the frenzy
and the Egyptian lily—

then let it go at that, he's safe, children, grandchildren
and a second wife.

XLIX

I wrote of course, congratulations and felicity,
a friend sent me the notice from a London paper,

Bridegroom of the Week, with the picture,
she smiled under a festive little hat,

her age? just young enough to be his daughter;
he looked older, rather commonplace, I thought;

the place? outside the official registrar;
the caption said, she wore sage green, was widow of one

of his former pilots, with a son,
how very suitable; he wrote a letter,

thanking me for mine, it was near Christmas,
and he enclosed the Christmas card from Lord-and-Lady,

and I sent back my card, addressed to both,
it was five years ago, and that was that.

L

It is not over, it has just begun; I read somewhere
in French I can't remember, only the word *semblables*,

that these "familiars" have the power of life and death
over each other; I think if I thought anything,

that I could help most with detachment and serenity,
"O, just keep out of it," I said when Christmas came,

and I could send a greeting with a Crown and Star,
something abstract, no angels at the manger,

O, wholly formal and in perfect taste,
and this made looking for my Christmas cards a game,

but no, I knew that I would never write,
"I'll never write again."

LI

I waited sixteen weeks and I was good,
at least, I think I was, "patience," they said,

"more patience" and "*Geduld*," they said, and Schwester Trude said,
"God wanted this, so you could have a rest";

I waited sixteen weeks and then was free, I thought,
"but at your age," they said, "the bone won't set,

you must go back to bed"; I said, "I'll try rebellion,"
for my prayers, I felt had failed;

I thought of you and then another picture came,
an article, Amico sent, "the usual thing," she wrote,

"the *au-delà* by your friend," and she enclosed
the cutting from the *Sunday Times*, your picture

and your comment on the other lives, Hell, Paradise,
and your pilots who were dead;

your friend? we've hardly named you through the years,
but you were there—and here—for suddenly,

I forged another prayer, hear me, O Master of the Air,
I cried, Light-bearer, pre-Adamic, Lucifer.

LII

Leave her, Elizabeth Dyer, the stage, the center,
she could walk, she could climb the attic stair,

could pray after a fashion, for a while anyway,
could invoke the past, could pore over the ancient books,

half guilty, half prophetic and half mad,
could believe in infinity and remember

how once her lover left the cup of sleep,
of death and of oblivion, within reach;

leave her, she can dream better than we,
remembering Sir Walter, she can see

further than we can see, can conjure up,
invoke, entreat, implore

the outline of an alabaster jar
and an Egyptian lily.

LIII

My friend, the river Thames ran past the door,
or not so far; barges and pageants now, for that was long ago,

the threat from Spain or somewhere else, the fire
that charred the warehouse and the priceless merchants' store

along the lower river; it ran a silver ribbon in the night,
you can't disguise the river, put out the light,

torch, lantern, brazier, lamp; crowd indoors by a candle,
you fortunate ones who can afford a candle;

wait, for your hour has come, O sinful city,
with a heretic upon the Throne, wait, for no watchman calls,

no voice is heard, and then the watchman woke
and the Lord God proclaimed, "your fate is in the balance,"

and the scales quivered and the seven weights showed
three one side, four the other, and the dark angels fell,

and the Apocalypse was clear to read,
not then in din and furor, but long after.

LIV

I mix my metaphors and history, my friend,
"I do not care for modern poetry," you wrote,

"I do not care for music or astrology"—why tell me that?
"I do not care for ceremonial"—and you gave a list,

all wrong, of what you called the rays, well, not wrong,
but illiterate or uninformed, the ray of healing

and the mental ray, I quite forget, but the impression
that you meant to give, remains, as of an amateur

dabbling in psychic matters, seriously but as a recreation,
do you see? you left the way open for discussion,

could you trap me, you would trap me,
but we trapped each other, it was a serious matter,

Circe—
Gyges...

LV

And what had I? the common courtesies of a wrecked world,
"another cup of tea—a cigarette?" "no, no—do you mind this?"

and he pulled out his pipe, "of course, not—smoke,"
he did not stuff tobacco in the bowl, he lounged in the big chair

and nursed his pipe, and all confusion vanished, it was home,
he could call up enchantment and enchanters, the hero of the
        moment

and all time, he was invisible but he was there;
I let the telephone ring on, ring on, I need not answer,

"but possibly, perhaps it is for you?" "no, no,"
nothing could spoil this moment, what we said

was immaterial, but we had to talk of something,
for the silence spoke of threat now past,

of the incalculable moment, when tense and resolute,
he flung the weight of "England's treasure," as he wrote of it,

into the balance and the balance swayed and hesitated,
and his heroic wings held and his wings beat back

the enemy, and in the silence there was all of this,
and of his thousand English pilots dead.

LVI

I am ashamed to speak of my predicament—
how long a prisoner? I who am so free,

my plight is nothing, I am fortunate;
"with bones like yours," the doctor said,

"so elegant, you can't expect a sudden miracle";
he did not say, "at seventy, it takes forever for a bone to heal";

and then there came the thought beyond the fear,
maybe there'll be a miracle, after all;

and then there came as answer to a prayer,
the thought, "maybe, I'll write a letter,"

I could simply say that I had read his article
and I could ask what else he'd written lately,

perhaps he'd like to hear, to know another
who'd traveled the same path, had got so far;

as far as what, as where? an arm-chair in a room,
a bed, a table, six months in Purgatory, no, not that,

five months perhaps, then this month, April,
with a breath from Paradise, when I seized my pencil

and my pencil wrote of the enchantment and the purple tent and how
following inexorable destiny, we met.

LVII

A sort of brusqueness and no nonsense,
but he liked the story; it was a game we played around a table,

Amico, a young Indian and his English mother;
I wrote of it after I heard him lecture and he wrote back,

it was the war of course and threat of death
that opened doors into this spirit-life;

I crowded with the rest to hear him speak,
he spoke casually, but it seemed sincerely;

our Indian friend had given me the ticket;
I squeezed in at the very last and thought,

how strange it was to hear him publicly,
speaking of messages and ghosts and spirits.

LVIII

The great days of the war had gone, we waited on,
he had retired; we had survived

the Battle and the threat of the invasion;
he seemed kind, fatherly and professorial;

one thought, he's not really talking down to us, an audience
who has faced annihilation with a joke

and cups of tea, common-or-garden English heroism,
girls in uniform and girls without, and older women,

rapt in ecstasy to hear the great and simple man
hold forth, talk to us in an easy friendly manner,

of people who were "here" and "there" as one,
stories and anecdotes, the sea, the Russian snow,

reports, he stated, given him by others,
automatic writers, mediums, extraneous matters,

no mention, it seemed odd, of his own men,
the part they played "before," what happened to them "after."

LIX

Our ancient vows—I lie alone—and everything is over—
no, not over, just begun—and if I think of Hugh,

it is the earlier England, I remember; I am forced
to think of things "before," in contrast to the "after,"

the venom and the anger, as of a Dragon standing guard
before a door—and I remember Hugh and how Sir Walter,

they said, had contact with daemonic powers and Spirits of the dead,
and this in only my comparison, who would accuse

the Master of the Air, the Air Marshal
who opened doors for many and for me—

and flung his hat and coat upon a chair,
and paced the floor and turned on me in fury . . .

and so remembrance brings us to this hour
in which I strive to save identity,

the Man—Angel or Devil—the *primum mobile*,
the mediator, destroyer and creator.

LX

And he was right and Hugh was right, "no woman
should explore these devious rites," how could I know

that he was Gyges and invisible, how could I know
that I was Circe with a secret key

and when the door swung open and was closed
swiftly, and he turned, the Dragon on the threshold,

in his fury, how could I know his fury was to save me,
that his repudiation was salvation.

LXI

Now you are old and tired and valiant, seventy-five a few days ago,
I wrote you for your birthday, once or twice,

for actually, I only knew you that one year,
though I had found you earlier through your lectures,

and we wrote and I sent messages from our Indian friend
and cards at Christmas and so on;

I followed out the guidance of *Alli*, so we called him,
or so he called himself or so his "guide," he said, had called him;

I find this is one of the over-seventy names of God,
seventy-two in fact, of which Elizabeth spoke;

I found her book in Lausanne on a shelf,
devoted to occult books, mostly French.

LXII

So I found your God-name or Elizabeth Dyer found it,
and your degree, thinking of your birthday,

Alla oddly, *Dieu adorable*, and mine not far
from yours, *Dieu qui inspire*, and *Teli*,

and there is *Alli*, *Dieu qui vivifie toute chose*,
your letters that he "read" me in the dark,

not knowing who had written them, not taking them from their
      envelopes,
with eyes closed, clairvoyantly seeing what the future held,

and "work" we had together, and some talk
of "a head off in the past," and of a monk

and of a being marked for some great destiny,
but longing for retirement and a time for contemplation and—a Ship;

the Ship was what inspired us, what brought *Alla* and *Teli*
to the ultimate goal of their ambitions and their hopes,

for it had come over and above the stresses and the fury and the fear,
bearing its priceless treasure,

"O, so many," *Alli* said, "shouting and laughing";
the Ship was for you.

LXIII

I like to think, to make the almost unbearable story bearable,
that Hugh was there, I like to think that the *Seaspray* returned,

with other phantom ships, to hail them as they fell,
and gather them together on that one mysterious Ship

that brought *Alla* and *Teli* together, that the miracle
extended through all time, but that eternity

was not a vast conception of philosophy,
but a simple plane, a near extension of our own common time,

where clocks tick and where no evil forces
shatter the continuity of young lives,

and where courtesy controls humanity,
and where the Master of the Air

says simply, "pride failed—
but all through time, I waited for you."

LXIV

Now will you laugh, my friend, I mean a cigarette,
this *near extension of our own common time*,

and chestnut spires, so lovely in the dusk,
I saw them and I breathed their anodyne,

but they come and close the window when the light is on,
for the *Maikäfer* bumps and zooms about my bed,

and he is hard to catch and the night-sister says,
"you can't have both, the open window and your table light";

so now I tell you this and now I'll reach
for cigarette and match, and this will be

my high philosophy (I know you'll understand),
remembrance of the seven times we met.

LXV

How could anything so complicated be so simple,
how could anything so difficult be so clear?

I mean "the cloud of witnesses" that worried us
as children and the Holy Ghost?

but strangely, it couldn't have happened, not to us,
without the good and bad of our predicament,

without Elizabeth, a sort of Marguerite to your Faust,
without the undercurrent that just didn't wreck us,

an invisible Circe or disguised Lilith,
or Helen, Guinevere, Semiramis,

that we invoke as Graces, even Virtues,
not for their beauty only, but for their implacable search

for the *semblable*, the haunting first cause,
the *primum mobile* that gave both Hell and Paradise to Dante;

perhaps, I boast, perhaps I should be cowed and disciplined,
a woman of seventy, lying—no—not helpless,

for I called for light,
and *Dieu qui inspire*, Light came.

LXVI

I should be too old for exaltation,
I am too old, but inexplicably,

spring threatens with enchantment
and I almost fear redemption through its beauty:

doors open, one door shut inexorably,
but I had sensed the depth and I was spared;

I traveled, I was happy, even although
the path had led from darkness

on through darkness, back to illumination,
and from illumination, to despair,

and from despair to inspiration,
and as answer to a prayer,

the *VALE AVE* and the thought beyond the fear,
perhaps there'll be a miracle, after all.

LXVII

Does *writing* equate *walking*?
well, here we are, my most august and dear Professor,

and my anxiety fades beside the contemplation
of your heroic suffering, and our meeting

in Vienna, when you were seventy-seven,
and our parting, some seven years later,

and the many threads woven into the father-image,
and the Oedipus riddle solved; and now waiting;

Geduld, Geduld, Geduld; "she must have patience,"
the last consultant said, "some of my cases

have to wait a year; we can later fortify
the pin, the wedge with a cross-wedge,

in three months possibly, but nature knows best,
better let her wait"—he was talking to Amico,

and she wrote, "'Patience, *Geduld*,' he says,
'why is she so impatient?'"

LXVIII

He might have been an ancient Cabalist,
none other than Ezra-Azriel returned, or another,

or many others, Socrates, of course;
O, he was sly and secret and revealed infinite secrets,

but the secrets kept were greater
than we dreamed of or dared dream;

I once apologized, "you must not think me superstitious,
but you seventy-seven" I said, "is eloquent;

I mean the number in itself"—and waited,
but he did not answer, he just let it go;

and once I had a dream-sequence of Houses and I said,
"I think it's astrological, a friend in England

sends me star charts and maps; this is outside
our work, I know; I mention it only

because of the dream sequence and the association
with your Star, Venus"; then he seemed to start

as if suddenly discovered and off guard, and said
with a sort of ironical amusement and half worship, "not *Venus*."

LXIX

Why do these words seem suddenly to laugh?
Onkelos, Hebrew? ("our uncle's book"),

or maybe it isn't Hebrew; I read of the *Targum de Jérusalem*,
attributed to *Onkelos*—is *Onkelos* Greek? no matter,

it is a question of *traditions transmises par la parole*,
and "Parole" is in Hebrew, *Kabalah*, and in French, *Kabal*;

so he honored his *parole*, I said,
meaning his personal word, his honor,

and maybe, there were other vows, impersonal, hieratic,
including whole cycles of lodges, Houses, cenacles,

and an oath is sacred, and the punishment, I read,
for revealing initiation secrets, may be death;

how could I laugh at this? I do not laugh—
witness, O Father, *Dieu, père secourable.*

LXX

I am frightened, I confess, to write of this,
and yet I flaunt the adventure, bear the secret

like a banner; I even laugh, or rather as I said,
the words laugh, though I added (slightly shivering,

following my pencil, slightly alarmed, wondering what would follow),
how could I laugh at this?

but there is laughter somewhere, far off at sea,
unconquerable, gay, heroic, unheard by us

but conveyed to us by *Alli*, and another sort of laughter,
sly, discreet and near, of another unconquered Spirit,

the Star of our Father, whose God-name, I find
is *Zaka* and whose attribute, *Dieu, père secourable.*

LXXI

He wrote in the end, that the messages were "frivolous,"
so Nemesis woke or Fate, symbolically wearing the crown

of metal spear points from the shattered lance staves,
a crown to be worn proudly, not easily set aside,

and a dark mourning robe over the fragile stuff,
the pleated linen hidden, the transparencies, semitransparencies

of the bride; yet even these words are inadequate,
for what happened, happened, it was a tour-de-force,

a trick of the hermetic "Joker" of the old alchemists,
no need to wonder why or how, or invoke Nemesis.

LXXII

Now there is only laughter, "O, so many," *Alli* said,
"shouting and laughing, and a name *Teli*,

Dieu qui inspire, and a bride; there is only now
and the hereafter, antithetical perhaps, but running side by side,

body and soul, spirit and body, the old problem,
the old pattern, complicated, simplified, translated and decoded,

Athens, Alexandria, Carthage, Rome, Freud—
he would have understood, followed the story

with admiration, sympathy, perhaps concern
lest I fall victim to abstract speculation,

or fall a victim to the Air Lord and his pride,
he would have felt the threat and the temptation,

he must have followed us, standing aside,
he must have hailed the Ship

that brought the messages, "Parole," the Word,
and added his breath to the breath of God.

LXXIII

Light follows darkness, and the darkness light,
the Dragon-lover of mythology was not chained in the pit,

Hannibal, Caesar, Martel,
but ploughed the earth inexorably,

and the sea, and last the *Dragon volant* sought the sky,
to inaugurate a new age and a new mythology,

a new Circe, Helen, Lilith;
what she sees, Helen, Semiramis, *Teli*,

is at best inadequate, fragmentary, but she saw *Alla*,
a whole, complete, armed for the divine event,

and unarmed when venomous before the threshold,
he turned to attack her, crowned.

LXXIV

There is *Alla*, *Teli* and our Indian friend, *Alli*,
there is *Zaka* unquestionably, and Amico

who sent me your last picture, is *Dieh*,
with the attribute, *Dieu qui délivrez des Maux*,

there are all the others, on earth, a "cloud of witnesses,"
as in heaven; may these deliver us

from all iniquity, questioning and distrust,
and at the last (I know they'll understand),

I ask for this, the blessing of the Ship, of the "Parole,"
in remembrance of the seven times we met.